THE COUNTRY CRAFT SERIES

PAPIER MACHÉ

PAPIER MACHÉ

Judi Smith

Bloomsbury Books
London

Previous page: A gilded setting with a pair of papier mâché candlesticks and a glossy black bowl decorated with pieces of shiny gold wrapping paper. The effect is rich and fun.

Published by Harlaxton Publishing Ltd
2 Avenue Road, Grantham, Lincolnshire, NG31 6TA, United Kingdom.
A member of the Weldon International Group of Companies.

First published in 1994

© Copyright Harlaxton Publishing Ltd
© Copyright design Harlaxton Publishing Ltd

This edition published in 1994 by
Bloomsbury Books
an imprint of
The Godfrey Cave Group
42 Bloomsbury Street, London. WC1B 3QJ
under license from Harlaxton Publishing Ltd.

Publisher: Robin Burgess
Editor: Dulcie Andrews
Illustrator: Sam Denley
Photographer: James Duncan
Typesetting: Sellers, Grantham
Colour separation: G A Graphics, Stamford
Produced in Singapore by Imago

British Library Cataloguing-in-Publication data.
A catalogue record for this book is available from the British Library.
Title: Country Craft Series: Papier Mâché
ISBN: 1-85471-442-2

4

CONTENTS

INTRODUCTION

Through this Country Craft series, it is our hope that you will find satisfaction and enjoyment in learning a new skill. In this case, that of working with papier mâché.

This craft has seen a revival due to modern pastes and paints which have made it a less messy and thus more enjoyable medium. Papier mâché may well conjure up images of a school classroom, or your mother's kitchen table with newspapers scattered on every surface, a bowl of mixing paste and brushes with sticky handles as you battled with the solid glue.

This book will erase those memories and show you how to handle the tools of one of the more simple, and certainly one of the most inexpensive, creative crafts. Look in the windows of even the most exclusive design stores and you will see an item made of papier mâché. You will not know it until you pick it up – the item will be lighter than you thought. Yet its colour and style will have led you to believe it was made of a more substantial material.

The current design trend in home accessories comes from designers interpreting colourful and exuberant South American imagery. With the wide variety of paint finishes now available – from soft marble effects through to high-gloss glazes – you can imitate the exuberant effect or choose a more sophisticated decorative finish.

Opposite: A jug and bowl set designed using the same pattern technique. The handle uses florists' wire for strength in the shape.

GETTING STARTED

BEFORE BEGINNING to learn the art of papier mâché, we should take a look at its long and fascinating history as people began creating papier mâché objects almost 300 years ago.

Paper itself was invented by the Chinese around AD 105 using the inner bark of the mulberry tree. They later experimented with paper pulp, incorporating a variety of other materials, such as discarded fishing nets, rags and rope to create unique effects. Legend suggests that the Chinese even created papier mâché helmets for their warriors to wear into battle. The skill of paper-making then spread west to the Middle East, Russia and on to Europe. It was the French who perfected the art of papier mâché; they also renamed the technique – a literal translation of the French is 'paper mulch'.

Two important factors leading to the popularity of papier mâché in 18th-century France were economy and ecology. Vast amounts of waste paper had begun to accumulate in large cities such as Paris, partly due to the increasing use of large advertising posters pasted up around the city. Paper was, at that time, a very expensive commodity so the obvious solution to the problem of waste was recycling. They simply added water to the torn paper to produce a pulp that was then packed into moulds. Papier mâché was allowed to dry and then was used in the manufacture of decorative objects, such as snuff and trinket boxes. These were, in turn, exported to the British market.

The British thought they could improve on the French technique and went on to build up a thriving papier mâché industry, providing employment for many people in the north of England. In addition, during the 18th century, there was an influx of beautiful Japanese lacquer work much admired by the British craftsmen. Papier mâché was a good medium to use for this particular 'look' but as the pulp was artificially dried in ovens and kilns, the final object often became distorted. This problem was overcome by Henry Clay in 1772 when he invented a new technique. Clay's process was simply to layer sheets of paper, glued on both sides, around a metal or wooden form, enabling the layers to dry slowly and evenly. The resulting objects would be smoother and therefore more suitable for use with the Japanese lacquer.

By the early 19th century the goods produced by one of the most popular papier mâché companies, Jenners and Betteridge, were in much demand and the industry thrived for a further 100 years. The Victorians used papier mâché in many original and decorative ways, producing furniture, chairs, clock cases, firescreens and even baby baths!

Opposite: The high gloss finish on these lacquered jars with lids look as if they are ceramic. In fact, they are made of papier mâché. The gloss finish creates the illusion.

The art of papier mâché has flourished in other parts of Europe: the Venetians in Italy have been fabricating carnival masks from the medium for years. The Spanish in Valencia have experimented and put papier mâché to exciting use in their folk festivals, sculpting large figures, some 3-4 metres (10-12 feet) high. They choose the best for the procession and sacrificially burn the others. In Mexico too on 'the day of the dead', buildings and streets are decorated with papier mâché skeletons and skulls as the people remember their loved ones in a joyous celebration of their previous life. However, it is the Indonesians and the Asians who are the main exporters of beautiful papier mâché work which can be a great source of inspiration.

Finally, it should be remembered that this versatile medium has been used by many 20th-century artists. Picasso was known to have produced work in a very similar vein under the name of 'papier déchiré'. Matisse and Braque went on to develop this method in their own unique styles. The medium of papier mâché has proved to be accessible, environmentally friendly and inexpensive.

PAPIER MÂCHÉ PROCESS

There are two techniques to build up a papier mâché object. The first is the 'layering' method, which is the easiest of the two. The layering method uses torn squares or strips of newspaper which are dipped into a glue mixture and then laid or wrapped over a plastic structure. A cardboard or wire armature could also be used for construction. The plastic bowl or structure should be covered with these sticky squares in layers and then left to dry somewhere warm and dust free.

The second is the 'pulp' method which needs to be either applied to a construction or packed into a mould. The pulp method also uses the torn paper but the pieces must be smaller and mixed with the glue in a bucket or large bowl. This mixture should be left overnight and then whisked to form a relatively smooth pulp. The pulp can then be packed into a mould and left to dry. It should be remembered that objects made using this method will take a longer time to cure due to the density of the pulp.

With the layering technique, it is important to layer approximately three coats and then allow to dry overnight. This craft is time consuming due to the drying time needed; it is, however, extremely rewarding and is well worth persevering with. It is advizable to have a few projects in progress at various stages, so you may continue working.

The pulp method is useful for more intricate work and can be used to sculpt and form faces or other extremities. The drying may take some time but the effects that can be produced are limitless; wonderful textures can be achieved with the addition of special paint effects. In the theatre world, papier mâché is used to imitate wood, rock, stone and many other solid materials at a fraction of the weight and cost.

COLLECTING PAPERS

All sorts of paper can be used to build up your object but the best are the broadsheet newspapers, due to their absorbency and durability. With the layering method, it is a good idea to have three different colours of newsprint available, as this will help you keep an account of the number of coats you have used. When the wet newspapers are applied they become translucent, so the different

Above: Many craftsmen adopted the delicate patterned styles being made in India during the 19th century. These antique trays feature mother of pearl inlay and combine lacquer and a gilt finish.

colours of newsprint help you to see that you have covered the object evenly.

Once you begin to collect decorative papers you will inevitably become addicted as there is such a fascinating selection available today. The choice is limitless: wrapping paper, sugar paper, napkins, newsprint, foils and packing papers to name just a few. Tissue and crêpe paper are wonderful as they can be overlaid with one another to create interesting additional colours, this process was often used in the work of Matisse.

As you begin to collect your paper, it is advizable to have in mind a theme or idea for your project, which can be as varied as a baroque urn, an art nouveau vase, a modernist bowl or a dinosaur. Paper itself can be a great source of inspiration. Hand-made papers often contain fibres, metal, leaves or bark – a wide variety of which are available at good art stores – and will provide unique effects on your finished articles.

This craft can become a compulsion, so you may find you start to scavenge for card and paper from all kinds of unexpected places, as wasted materials abound in this 'throwaway' society. The junk mail that comes through the mail-box on a daily basis can be put to good use in a pulp. So can cardboard packaging used for breakfast cereals.

PAPER THICKNESS

The amount and thickness of the layers for your projects can vary enormously depending on the design or effect required. For an average bowl, an approximate number of layers would be ten, including the final decorative paper layer and inside coating. Obviously, when using cardboard as a base, fewer layers are needed.

If a more delicate effect is desired, a high percentage of the PVA glue must be added, as it strengthens the structure and adds plasticity; this will produce a stronger but thinner membrane to be used, perhaps, for a lampshade or mobile. With the pulp method, this mixture can be loaded on to a constructed cardboard base or mould at a depth of 2.5cm (1 inch) and then dried thoroughly before the next mass is added. It is surprising how firm these products become after they are dried and, once an item is thoroughly dry, it will be extremely light to pick up and handle.

When constructing a larger item such as a jug or column, it is essential to build up the layers gradually but to a much vaster extent, eventually layering up to 15-20 coats.

With experience, it will become much easier to select good strong papers that will bond together and help you to build your masterpiece and, as you gain confidence in the craft, you will develop a feel for the number and thickness of layers required.

PAINTING AND STENCILLING

Once your item is thoroughly dry, decoration can take place. You must think about where the object is going to be placed or who it is going to be given to, as this will help you to decide on colour and decoration.

A coat of primer or emulsion will give you a good base. When painting, use very soft brushes as they can reach all the crevices and bumps that may have appeared. Water-based paints are good for even coverage and depth of colour, although a spirit-based varnish will

Fig. 1. Tape the stencils in place with masking tape then stipple the paint through with a stubby brush.

Above: A large sun symbol created from an Indonesian design was created using the pulp method.

have to be used as it will not disturb the paint. The spirit-based paints do give a good and even coverage but they must be used in well-ventilated areas. Acrylic paints are another good medium; they can be used with water, or mixed with turpentine to give a denser consistency.

Paint can be applied with a brush, a sponge or sprayed on with an aerosol; the latter is extremely useful when painting the insides of urns or jugs. When using metallic paint in powder form, it is easier to apply if mixed with

varnish. Marbling is also an attractive way to cover your objects.

Stencilling can be used very effectively, particularly if gold or silver is used on a dark background. The stencils can be traced from a pattern, wallpaper or material and then cut out from oiled card. (Make oiled card by rubbing cooking oil into light card. This protects it from the paint and makes it more flexible.) The stencil can then be attached to the object and paint stippled through the cut-out shapes (Fig. 1).

DIFFERENT MATERIALS

In this book we will be dealing mainly with paper. However, once the basic technique has been mastered, you can go on to experiment with the techniques and incorporate other materials to create interesting effects.

Corrugated cardboard can be used to build up a solid structure, as can wire mesh on a larger piece. For handles or other extremities, corrugated cardboard can be strengthened with wire to form intricate coils and curves. Polystyrene can be incorporated to create feet on a bowl or urn. In fact, the versatility of polystyrene is exceptional, as a hot wire or knife can be used to sculpt the material into interesting shapes as a former; the papier mâché can then be applied in layers as an outer coating.

Any discarded object can be used as a former or mould, either to be removed or to remain inside. Old plastic vases become newly desirable as they are transformed into gold-encrusted vessels. A cigar box could be dramatically changed into a jewel box with just a small amount of imagination.

Different finishes can be achieved by using coloured inks, paints, metallic spray paints, tissue papers or wrapping papers. Foils, gold leaf and burnishing are other treatments that create unique effects. The use of materials to create textures can have amazing effects: for instance, string, shells, gems and studs glued on to a piece make it unique.

The process of papier mâché is relatively simple although, like any craft, it takes time to become familiar with the basics. Once you have become confident, your imagination has a free rein to experiment with other variations and combinations.

DESIGN IDEAS

Ideas for this craft are limitless but you may find that a smaller item is best to start with, until a real feel for the craft takes over.

As a source of inspiration you could refer to books on particular artists such as Picasso or Salvador Dali. Furniture and design history can be enlightening; look at shapes, structure and textures. Look out for modern examples of papier mâché from the Far East. India, Nepal and Indonesia produce an extensive array of products which are exported all around the world.

In the reign of Queen Victoria a vast number of papier mâché objects were produced, so search out books on this era. Toys from this period are of particular interest, as many dolls and puppets were beautifully made of papier mâché. Visit local art galleries and museums as you may well find excellent examples of papier mâché there.

Folk art is another great area to research into. You will find that many symbols, for example the sun and moon, have great significance; they were worshiped by tribes such as the Incas and the Aztecs and are supposed to bring good fortune.

Papier mâché is an extremely versatile and tactile craft which people of all ages can experiment with. The 'Beginner's Project' demonstrates a selection of objects, complete with a step-by-step guide to start you off. Once you have completed your first piece you will find you are already planning the next.

Opposite: A selection of early 19th century patterned boxes with roses and daisies illustrates the fine art of decoration which was prevalent in that era.

Tools and Materials

ART AND CRAFT STORES now stock a comprehensive range of materials for papier mâché enthusiasts, from the complete beginner to the professional. If in doubt about a product, ask the store manager for advice.

Tools such as scissors, craft knives and brushes should be of a high standard. The quality of the glue is very important; the dried paste should be a recognized brand and the PVA glue must be strong and water soluble.

A sharp craft knife or scalpel will help with the intricacies of the more difficult cutting when dealing with edges and handles. Thin florist's wire (floral wire) and cutters are necessary when strengthening handles or legs. Wire mesh to build up large armatures is both light, strong and cheap.

Plastic moulds are best for basic shapes, as they are light, moveable and more pliable when removing work. Balloons provide a good base for large more convex work and they can be hung up to dry easily.

Fine sandpaper with blocks can be used for sanding down bumps to create a smoother finish. Polyurethane varnish for the outer coat can be either gloss or matt. You will find the varnish enhances the colours of the object, giving it a more professional look. The varnish comes as a spirit- or water-based liquid. If the object is painted, it is best to use the spirit-based varnish, which also provides a water-proof base for items that are going to hold food, such as a fruit bowl. The water-based varnish does form a reasonably good coating and is more environmentally friendly. The list of basic requirements is as follows:

- Newspaper (in three different colours)
- PVA glue (water soluble which dries clear)
- Wallpaper paste (dried)
- Scissors (long blades)
- Sharp craft knife or scalpel
- Brushes
- Fine sandpaper and block
- Corrugated cardboard
- Florist's wire (floral wire)
- Wire cutters
- Clear gloss varnish
- Metallic spray paint
- Paint (water- or spirit-based) and primer or matt emulsion
- Tissue paper
- A selection of wrapping papers
- Damp cloth
- Mineral turpentine
- Re-usable adhesive
- Vaseline (to grease mould)
- Balloons (for moulding)
- Wire mesh
- Plastic bowls
- Brown gum strip
- Masking tape
- String
- Modelling clay or plasticine

Opposite: A collection of materials that you will need to begin creating papier mâché.

STARTING WORK

A FIRM IDEA from your research will be a positive start to the final papier mâché article. A good sense of colour and shape are important, along with a vague idea of size to calculate the amount of materials needed.

SOURCES

Papers
Interesting papers can be gathered from a vast array of places; art stores stock a wide range of tissue, crêpe and wrapping papers. Newsagents and gift stores are also a good source. You will probably find you have enough newspapers at home to begin the process with. Magazines, as long as they are the newspaper type (too glossy and they become less absorbent), provide brightness and variety. Old books can be recycled into a variety of magnificent objects. Laser copies are good for adding colour and interest.

Moulds
These can be very simple, just a plastic mixing bowl or container that has an interesting shape. Balloons, although you may associate this method with school children, are a very versatile basis for papier mâché work. Modelling clay or plasticine is an excellent material for papier mâché as it can be rolled and modelled to create very wonderful effects. When making objects such as puppets or dolls, the heads can be created by moulding papier mâché over the clay. The papier mâché is then cut off and reformed to provide a complete head which is both light and interesting. Clay can also be used to create mouldings for vases or urns in the same way. This process can give the impression that an article is far more intricate than it actually is which is why theatres and circuses use papier mâché so often.

Cardboard can be added at a later stage to extend and decorate items – by creating plinths, curved lids or elaborate handles you can transform an ordinary plastic bowl into an 'objet d'art'.

Other materials
Venture into your garden shed or garage for discarded packaging and wire mesh. The various types of paint you may find about the home can transform your work into something really eye catching. Metallic car spray gives a lustrous finish, while matt black creates the illusion of weight and density.

Build up a collection of odd bits and pieces – things like bells, gems, buttons, shells, string and pressed flowers – which can be incorporated into the final decoration of your work. You may find that old discarded junk can be very successfully recycled into many exotic-looking treasures that will be admired and marvelled at especially when you own up to their origins.

Opposite: A modern wastepaper bin made from a cardboard base is a good example of how professional papier mâché can be made to look.

STORING

A completely dry, warm environment is needed not only to store the paper and card to build the object but to help dry out the layers thoroughly. A trunk or large box, stored in a dry place, will help keep your papers, card and other bits and pieces together. Materials like wire can remain in the garage or loft. The wet articles will do best in an airing cupboard or by a radiator or boiler to speed their drying.

WORK AREA

Try to have a designated work area if possible. The workspace should have good natural light, with access to a lamp if necessary. It should also have good ventilation and be relatively dust free. The table should be protected with plastic and a good comfortable chair will help to make papier mâché a pleasurable experience. Ideally, it should be a place where you can safely leave work in progress and you should have easy access to the drying area, as moving the 'wet work' can be quite nerve wracking.

When drying, you must make sure that everyone in the household is aware of the wet model and that it cannot be knocked or damaged in any way. Try to store the wet work up on a high shelf, making sure it is not touching anything else. While drying, it must be possible for the work to be left overnight and not moved. The longer time you leave between layers, the stronger the objects will become (Fig. 2).

Fig. 2. When drying the item, try to stand the object on small supports, for example, yogurt cartons to ensure good circulation of air and an even drying process.

Opposite: For cat-lovers, this Egyptian-style feline is the perfect decorative companion.

Above: An urn in the Grecian style is easy to make. To make it perfect, pay particular attention to the handles when finishing the project.

TECHNIQUES OF THE CRAFT

THE BASIC TECHNIQUES for creating a beautiful piece of papier mâché are not too difficult to learn. This chapter explains in detail the techniques needed to prepare a mould or construction ready for work and then goes on to describe the stages involved in the unique process of papier mâché.

PREPARING THE MOULD

You must be sure the surface of the mould is clean and totally regular, then you should grease the surface with vaseline. When using a convex mould, plastic film can be wrapped around the mould as a substitute for the vaseline (Fig. 3). In the case of a concave mould, for example a jelly mould, it is essential to work the grease into all the cracks and creases to be sure the article can be released easily when thoroughly dry.

If a corrugated structure is to be used, it must be cut, rolled and firmly taped ready for the layers or pulp to be applied. Depending on the final effect expected, the cardboard method cuts down the number of layers and the overall drying time (Fig. 4).

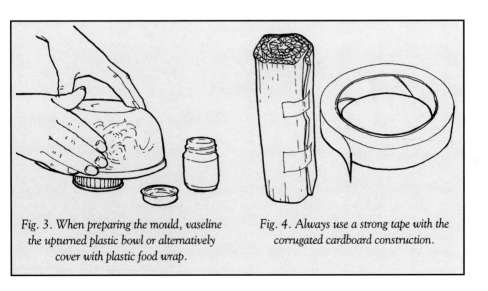

Fig. 3. When preparing the mould, vaseline the upturned plastic bowl or alternatively cover with plastic food wrap.

Fig. 4. Always use a strong tape with the corrugated cardboard construction.

Next page: A selection of decorative and useful papier mâché objects created by using various techniques of the craft.

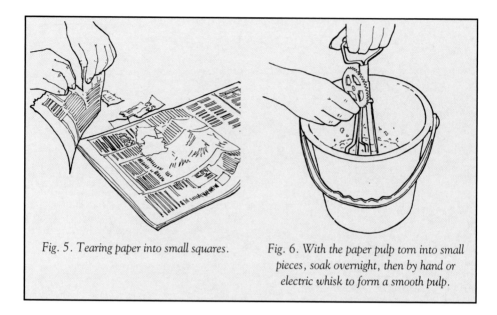

Fig. 5. Tearing paper into small squares.

Fig. 6. With the paper pulp torn into small pieces, soak overnight, then by hand or electric whisk to form a smooth pulp.

CONSTRUCTION

There are no limits to the size you can make a construction; it could be anything from a life-size cat to the Statue of Liberty! This medium lends itself well to large projects as the cost is low and the materials are easily accessible. An additional bonus is that even large objects remain surprisingly weightless.

When a large construction is required, wire mesh is the best base to use due to its versatility and strength. Wooden struts can be added to reinforce a structure, particularly if height is needed. The papier mâché can then be layered over the model to create a smoother coating, which will in turn dry to produce a solid model.

Corrugated cardboard can be found in most homes and is a great material to start building up a project. It can be glued, taped and folded up into a solid structure that can then be covered with the papier mâché. The cardboard must be secured by tape or strong glue so it retains its shape while the pulp is applied. As the pulp dries, it will encase the cardboard as part of the model itself. Cardboard works particularly well on articles such as frames for mirrors and pictures.

Handles can be cut from the corrugated cardboard and reinforced with florist's wire (floral wire) to form curls and twists. The wire will also help to keep the shape of the handles, as the wet papier mâché can distort the shape before it dries. It is best to make the handles and feet separately and then add them to the main body of the object. Glue and tape them separately, then add more papier mâché mixture to blend the edges into the article.

Polystyrene is a good former for pedestals and legs and can easily be cut and incorporated into the papier mâché project.

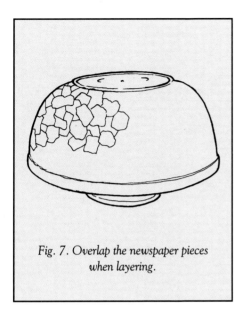

Fig. 7. Overlap the newspaper pieces when layering.

MIXING GLUES & TEARING PAPER

After the mould or construction has been prepared, the paper tearing should begin. When working on a very convex object, use layers of small squares. On a large construction you can use larger strips to bind around. The paper disappears at an alarming rate so it is best to build up a large stock.

Paper itself has a grain and the way to find its natural grain is to tear lengthways then across and examine the edges; this is particularly relevant if your final coating is a dark paper. When paper is torn against the grain it will be harder to tear and may have a white edge: in reverse, it will separate in longer strips with no change of colour to its edge. Paper should always be torn, not cut. Cut edges appear too sharp and they are harder to blend when layering (Fig. 5).

Care must be taken when mixing the glue,

as the proportions will effect the hardness of the finished article. Wallpaper paste mixed with water (according to the manufacturer's instructions) in a large jar would need one part PVA (water soluble) to six parts paste. If a strong but translucent effect is desired add an extra 25 per cent glue. The PVA glue is a little more expensive than the paste, so only use these proportions on a particularly important piece of work.

If there is any glue left over it can be kept in a jar until it is needed the next time. To make pulp, small pieces of torn paper must be mixed with the glue in a bucket or large bowl. The mixture should be left overnight and then whisked, using a metal egg whisk, to form a relatively smooth pulp (Fig. 6). Pulp must be kept damp and cool until it is neeed.

LAYERING METHOD

This method is the easiest. Using the torn squares of paper, you simply dip the pieces into the glue mixture and layer them on to the mould or balloon (Fig. 7). The first application will be the most difficult but, as you persevere, the process becomes relaxing and absorbing – enjoy the sensation of the smoothing of the layers. When mixing the glue, it is advizable to use warm water to help you overcome the shock of wet hands (although gloves can be used). The glue can be applied with a brush but, with practice, just having a damp cloth nearby will suffice.

The mould can be slightly raised by placing a can or tin underneath so it can be turned without disturbing the layers. On the first project four coats of papier mâché should be sufficient before you leave the object to dry overnight. As you become more confident with the craft, you will instantly recognise the

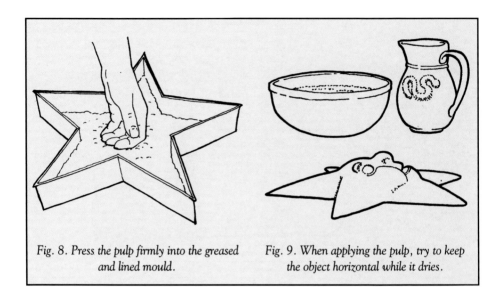

Fig. 8. *Press the pulp firmly into the greased and lined mould.*

Fig. 9. *When applying the pulp, try to keep the object horizontal while it dries.*

amount of wet layers you can cope with.

The use of different coloured newspapers is important for your first encounter, to help you keep a note of the layers you have completed. You will need to cover the object with approximately 10-15 layers, with be-tween three to five rest periods for drying the separate stages. The layering method can also be used to attach handles and feet and to blend in patterns and form textures.

PULP METHOD

This technique is most successful when used on a large object. After the torn paper has been soaked overnight with the glue mixture, it should be whisked and may then be applied to the mould or construction.

Pulp is easiest to control in a mould. It should be poured into the mould and then

pressure can be applied to squeeze out excess liquid (Fig. 8). A depth of no more than 5cm (2 inches) of pulp should be applied at any one time. Drying time will be between 12 to 24 hours, depending on the drying conditions and the thickness of the layers you have applied. All objects must be thoroughly dried out before being released from their moulds or they will start to break up. The drying of moulds should never be rushed as this causes bubbling and distortion. The weight of the object will change dramatically from the wet process to the dry and this can be a useful guide as to whether the article is ready.

When used on a construction, pulp will need to be applied with more care and precision in thinner layers as the drying can take longer. If, for example, the pulp is being used to form a face it can be shaped and

Opposite: The three-legged bowl shown here makes a perfect container for treasured decorations.

moulded and left to dry horizontally (Fig. 9), if possible. When working on a vertical structure, you may need to add more PVA glue to the initial mixture and apply the pulp in small amounts, drying the article between coats.

Marvellous textures can be achieved with the pulp by using a selection of tools; knitting needles can create grooves and pastry cutters can be pressed into a mass to remove sections.

REMOVING BUBBLES & BLEMISHES

If the papier mâché process is rushed at any time you may find that the layers bubble. Do not panic; this can be rectified. Once the bubble is located, a small cut or incision should be made and pure PVA glue worked into the area until the layers start to adhere.

Objects made with the pulp method can sometimes develop a rough surface when dry but this can easily be resolved by sanding with fine sandpaper. Once the exterior is dry sanding can commence until the desired smoothness is achieved.

Rough or uneven edges can be delicately trimmed with a sharp scalpel and then layered over to create a fine straight finish.

Large dents can be built up with extra pulp and layered over. It is sometimes necessary to feel for dents or dips as they may not show up easily to the naked eye. Papier mâché is a tactile, sensuous craft and you must learn to involve your senses, particularly sight, touch and hearing. When you check a bowl to see if it is dry, it will make a hollow sound when tapped; if there are any weaknesses in the structure, they can be found by tapping the object all over and listening for the sound

changes. You will soon learn to detect a blemish without a second thought.

SANDING

When the object has totally dried out it can be sanded. Only start this process if you are sure that at least four layers have been used – any less and the object would be too flimsy. During the layering process you may have noticed that small bumps and folds have appeared. This is not a major disaster as they can be smoothly removed with fine sandpaper. It is best to use the finest paper as this will just remove the crease or bump without disturbing the rest of the layers on the surface.

Try to maintain an even pressure while sanding. Try also to resist the temptation of rushing this process as carelessness can cause even more damage. If the paper begins to tear, it must be removed at once with a sharp craft knife or scalpel. You must then work some PVA glue into the cut to prevent it from pulling away again.

Handles or curved objects such as feet will need extra care and patience. You must sand these only when you are sure they are firmly glued in place and are totally dry. Experience will help you decide when to begin sanding and how long to sand for. You must pay attention when sanding particularly thin objects as these can so easily be damaged.

A damp cloth should be used to wipe up the dust from both the object and surrounding surfaces in preparation for the next coat of papier mâché. If the next stage is to varnish, be extra meticulous with dust removal as this can interfere with the final coat.

Opposite: The most ordinary lamp base can be transformed by using metallic and textured paper to create an interesting and creative effect.

Finishing Techniques

AT THIS STAGE the real fun begins. The imagination can now run riot and lavish effects can be indulged. There is a vast array of materials to choose from to create your final unique piece. Gold paint, shells, patterned wrapping papers and string are just a few ideas to think about.

SPECIAL EFFECTS

Decorative wrapping papers applied as the final layer can change the whole look of an article, as a newspaper-covered construction becomes an elegant rose-covered bowl with gold edges and feet.

Tissue paper applied in small pieces and overlaid in different shades will transform your object. A word of warning when using tissue paper – some of the stronger-coloured tissues may stain your hands. However, the stain will only last for a couple of days.

Feathers, shells, gemstones or sequins glued in place or arranged in a design can be used to construct an interesting collage. String can be wound around handles or lids to add texture.

Acrylics or poster paints are a cheap and immediate way to create lavish symbols or flowers. Maybe you could paint in the style of a particular artist, for example Andy Warhol. Metallic paints, used with imagination, can completely change the appearance of an article, giving it density, body and lustre. By masking off areas and spray-painting, a professional finish is achieved, particularly if colours are to merge and be overlaid.

(Remember, spray paints must only be used in a well-ventilated area.) Stencils and spray paints work very well together enabling you to create wonderful effects quite effortlessly. See also 'Painting and Stencilling' (p.12) for more tips and ideas.

To marble your object, fill a suitable bucket or bowl with water, float oil paints on the top and simply dip your object in. This technique can produce some dramatic and unusual effects.

Even gold leaf and verdigris processes can be applied to the papier mâché; the medium seems to have no limits. Let your imagination and sense of adventure take over as you experiment with new techniques and designs. Then once these have been successfully produced and thoroughly dried, you can proceed to the varnishing stage.

INSIDES, HANDLES & EXTREMITIES

The insides and undersides of objects are as important as the exteriors. A neglected inside can detract from all the effort and imagination that has gone into the exterior of the object.

Spray paint is the easiest option for jugs, vases and urns. (Be sure if using this method to spray in a well-ventilated area.) The spray method can also be used for bowls. Tissue is

Opposite: A jewellery box with lid made in the style popular in India

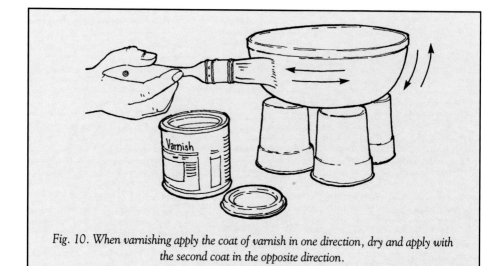

Fig. 10. When varnishing apply the coat of varnish in one direction, dry and apply with the second coat in the opposite direction.

an effective material to use inside a bowl, particularly if you pick out a complementary colour from the decorative paper used on the outside of the bowl. Matt emulsion can be poured into a jug or urn, swished around and then poured out to leave an even, single-colour coating.

Handles can be extremely lavish or simply painted. String can produce excellent effects and gems or shells glued in place and then painted gold look wonderful. Feet and handles must be tightly secured in place, painted then varnished to seal them. Wire can be threaded through the foot or handle and on to the item for extra reinforcement. Wire and corrugated cardboard can be used to create very interesting effects. If the card is then cut with the corrugations running vertically, the thin wire

can be threaded through and then curled up with a twist; this treatment works very well on the handles of a baroque urn, for example.

The undersides of objects can be painted in a complementary or contrasting shade or they can be covered in wrapping paper or découpage before being sealed with varnish. Metallic doilies or felt are interesting ideas for alternative materials for bases.

VARNISHING

Once your object has been fully dried and beautifully decorated you may proceed to the varnishing to finish and seal.

Your choice of varnish will depend on you as an individual and the project you are undertaking. There are two types: the more environmentally-friendly varnish is water-

Opposite: Gold is enticing, especially when used as a finish on a cheerful sun-face which can hang on a wall in any room.

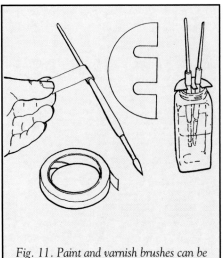

Fig. 11. Paint and varnish brushes can be left suspended in a bottle (i.e. a baby's bottle) to prevent the bristles from distorting.

conditions. The brushstrokes of one coat should always be in one direction but should alternate between each coat: for example, from left to right for the first coat then allow to dry, then from top to bottom for the next coat and so on (Fig.10). Your work area should be dust free, with good ventilation and lighting. The surface should be protected with polythene. Raise the object off the bench slightly by balancing it on a large tin or can. This helps to prevent it from sticking to the bench and an unsightly ridge forming around its base or edge. Make a note of the direction you are varnishing in so, if you are interrupted, you can resume the process in the same direction.

Keep a jar of either water or turpentine (depending on the type of varnish you are using) to dip brushes into if you have to stop at any time. Between coats the varnish brush can be left in the jar but it must be suspended so the bristles remain straight and do not pick up any of the sediment at the bottom of the fluid. After use, clean brushes in either water or turpentine, wash them in a mild liquid detergent, then dry them thoroughly before putting them away. Clean brushes are essential for a good finish and thorough cleaning prolongs the life of the brush (Fig.11).

Remember that damp or humid conditions will prolong the drying process. Do not attempt to rush the varnishing process, as hurried drying will result in cloudy varnish. It is also advizable to leave the article to dry with air circulating all around – stand the object on top of a tin can or plastic carton.

based, which dries quickly, and the other is spirit-based which cures a little harder. If decorating with a water-based paint, you must use the spirit-based varnish. Spirit-based varnish should also be used for objects which are going to hold food as it is more durable.

There are several schools of thought as how many coats are necessary: only you can really decide when you think the object has had enough. However, three to six coats (depending on the thickness of the object) are usually regarded as a minimum guide.

Coats should be applied in smooth even strokes and allowed to dry overnight or for 24 hours, depending on the environmental

Opposite: The star candle set shown in the photograph makes an impressive tableau and is suitable for any room in your home.

Beginner's Project

ONCE YOU have studied the procedures described in the previous chapters, you will be ready to start on your first project.

This project consists of three objects, individually not very ambitious but, when they are all completed, they join together to make an impressive set. We are going to produce a candlestick with a cardboard-structured centre and papier mâché over the outside. The second item is a jug with a balloon as its base and cardboard additions. Papier mâché is used to build it up to its full capacity. The final object is a simple bowl, made around an inexpensive plastic mixing bowl and then decorated imaginatively.

Layering will be the predominant method used in this project.

MATERIALS
- Corrugated cardboard
- A balloon
- A plastic mixing bowl
- Wallpaper paste and PVA glue
- Scissors and scalpel or craft knife
- Newspaper in three colours
- Florist's wire (floral wire)
- Brown gum strip
- Wrapping paper
- Small piece of thick card
- Metallic spray paint
- Polyurethane spirit-based varnish

- Sandpaper
- Vaseline

Care and patience will be needed for the first project although, once it is completed, there will be no holding you back.

STEP ONE
Candlestick
Prepare your cardboard structure. Carefully cut out a rectangle of corrugated cardboard approximately 20cm (8 inches) by 35cm (14 inches). Roll it up and stick it together to form a long tube. Cut out four circles 7.5cm (3 inches) in diameter, and glue just two of them together. Measure the circumference of the tube and, using this measurement, cut another two lengths of cardboard to a depth of 4cm (1½ inches). These two lengths are collars to stick around the ends of the main tube to support the circles. When sticking the collar to the top end of the tube, overlap the edge as this will create a cavity for the candle to sit in. Once the collars are stuck in place, attach the two glued-together circles to the bottom of the tube to from a secure base. Measure the circumference of the top end and draw a circle of the same size right in the centre of the two extra cardboard circles. Cut out the inner circle and push the cardboard rings down over the top of the collar to form a crown which should be firmly glued in place.

Opposite: A trio in gold and white suitable for a stunning table decoration at a dinner party. The inside of the bowl and the jug are painted gold for effect.

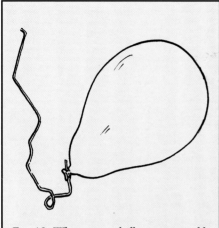

Fig. 12. When using a balloon as a mould, be sure to tie the end with string to enable the balloon to be hung up to dry.

You can cut into these two circles to form a star shape. This construction may take quite a time to build but, once it is formed, it is simple to apply the papier mâché on top.

Jug

Blow up a balloon carefully. It is better to use the biggest balloon possible as it will not need to be blown up to its full capacity – too much air can cause too much pressure and it may explode. The balloon will need to be greased with vaseline; make sure the whole surface is covered. Tie a string to the knot – this will make it easier to hang up and dry (Fig.12).

Bowl

Search out a good well-shaped plastic bowl, making sure it does not have too much of a ridge which could cause problems when separating the mould from the bowl. The bowl should also be greased thoroughly. As an alternative to the vaseline, thin plastic food wrap can be used to provide a good barrier between the mould and papier mâché.

STEP TWO

Collect together a variety of coloured newspapers – preferably three colours – and store them in a plastic bag to keep them dry. Search out a plastic tub with a lid (perhaps an empty ice cream container) to mix and store your glue. Check the packet details on the wallpaper paste as these vary considerably from brand to brand. Mix up the wallpaper paste in the tub, using approximately 600ml (1 pint) of warm water, until it is of the consistency of double cream. The PVA glue will now need to be mixed in; you will need one part PVA to six parts wallpaper paste. When the PVA glue is added, it should cloud the clear wallpaper paste to a creamy-white colour – this is an indication that the correct amount has been added.

The papers must be torn into 5cm (2 inch) squares, keeping the different colours separate. Make sure you have a considerable pile of pieces prepared as they will be used up at an alarming rate when you begin working.

Candlestick

Rub the mixed glue into the surface of the cardboard structure. Dip a couple of the torn squares into the glue, scrape off the excess using the side of the tub and apply the paper

Opposite: For the project you need: a balloon blown up to this size; newspaper, a wide plastic bowl. vaseline jelly, string and tape.

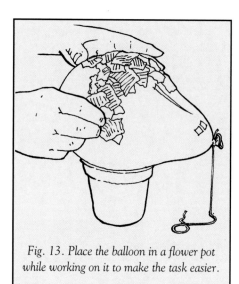

Fig. 13. Place the balloon in a flower pot while working on it to make the task easier.

completely covered. Once you have covered the whole balloon smoothly, swap to another colour of newspaper and continue this process until you have completed three coats. The balloon may be difficult to control and it can be helpful to use a large flower pot to contain the balloon, with a stone or weight in the bottom of it to hold down the string (Fig.13). After three coats leave to dry overnight.

Bowl

Place the greased bowl upside-down on a large tin so it sits securely away from the surface of the table. Again, dip the newspaper squares into the glue mixture and start to layer on to the bottom of the bowl. Overlap the squares, making sure the whole surface is completely covered. If you find when applying the papier mâché that the mixture begins to sag or slide because it is too wet, simply apply dry squares to the wet layers and this will help to bind the mixture together. Using one colour of newspaper at a time, continue until you have applied three even coats. The bowl can then be left to dry overnight until the colour lightens and the weight decreases.

to the candlestick. Make sure the squares are layered evenly and smoothly, as this will cut down on the sanding later on. When applying paper over the circular base, use thinner, smaller pieces to prevent heavy folds; this is also necessary when gluing around the points of the top star. When the article is completely covered, repeat the process with a different coloured newsprint until you have applied three coats evenly. Leave to dry overnight

Jug

The first coat is difficult to apply but it is worth the effort. With the greased balloon on its string, start to layer the glued squares from the top down to the string. The wet squares must be overlapped to be sure the surface is

STEP THREE

The next stage is just a matter of checking the surfaces of the objects to make sure there are no unsightly bumps or folds. If there are, just sand them gently away with fine sandpaper (Fig.14).

If you are satisfied with the feel of the surface, the layering process can continue. Remember to start with the same colour of

The second stage of the project needs plenty of newspaper to build up a firm foundation. Any additions – handles or a base – should be glued into place using cardboard as a "former", then use layers of papier mâché over the top of the "former".

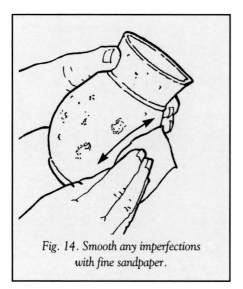

*Fig. 14. Smooth any imperfections
with fine sandpaper.*

the balloon and start to build up its structure. Cut out two cardboard strips approximately 4cm (1½ inches) by 30cm (12 inches). Join the ends together to form two rings. One ring should be glued to the bottom of the jug to make a base and the other to the top to make a rim. The structure will need to be cut into to incorporate the top ring. Papier mâché over these rings to form a solid base and a smooth rim – you may need to use two coats.

Bowl

If the bowl feels smooth and quite solid it can be freed from its mould. The inside will now need attention to ensure that it is firm and well glued. Add another three coats then return the bowl to the mould to dry.

STEP FIVE
Candlestick

This should be almost ready for decoration. Check it very carefully and sand and repair where necessary.

Jug

Thoroughly check the surface, paying particular attention to the joined pieces to see that they have amalgamated evenly. Feel the surface for any irregular bumps or folds and correct them if necessary

Now you must decide where you would like the spout to be placed and cut a 'V' shape using your craft knife or scalpel, into the top rim approximately 2.5cm (1 inch) deep. Draw a triangle on thick card 4cm (1½ inches) deep by 5cm (2 inches) across and cut it out. Fold this triangle in half and tape into the 'V' shaped cut; this may need some adjustment, so try several different positions until you are satisfied with the look of the jug. For the

newsprint that you began with in Step One.

The candlestick will possibly only need two more coats. The bowl and jug will benefit from an extra three coats. In the case of the jug, do not be alarmed if the balloon has gone down: just remove the old balloon and re-place with a fresh one, blowing it up inside the shell. You will only need the balloon for these stages; once the next three coats have been applied the shell should be firm enough to work on without its support.

Leave all the items to dry overnight.

STEP FOUR
Candlestick

Again, check its surface. If you can still feel the ridges of cardboard underneath continue with another layer.

Jug

This should now be firm enough to remove

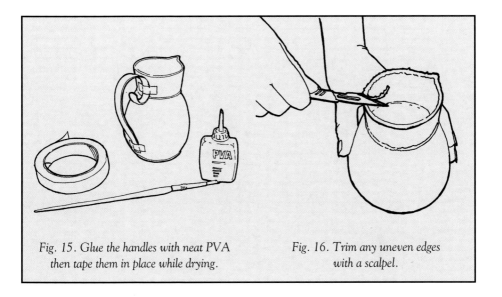

Fig. 15. Glue the handles with neat PVA then tape them in place while drying.

Fig. 16. Trim any uneven edges with a scalpel.

handle, cut out a corrugated cardboard strip 2.5cm (1 inch) by 20cm (8 inches). Make sure the strip is cut along the corrugations to allow wire to be threaded along the ridges. The handle can now be curled up and attached with gummed tape to the side of the jug. Papier mâché must now be layered over the lip and handle to ensure that they are securely attached. Leave all this to dry thoroughly overnight.

Bowl

Once you are satisfied with the look of the bowl, additions such as feet or handles will need to be considered. Any additions should be stuck in place either with gummed tape or pure PVA then left to dry before a layer of papier mâché can be applied (Fig. 15).

STEP SIX

If you are pleased with the completed objects, this stage is where the real fun begins. The patterned wrapping paper should be torn and ready for the final coating; remember the glossier type of paper will need a longer soaking in the glue.

Cover the jug and bowl with the patterned paper layer, making sure the surfaces are completely covered and smooth to touch. Pay particular attention to edges and attached pieces such as handles and feet. Check edges and trim with a scalpel or craft knife. Leave to dry overnight (Fig. 16).

Spray the insides with metallic paint. Use these sprays in a well-ventilated area with a background of newspaper to protect the surrounding surfaces. To cover the whole item, spray the bottom first, leave it to dry for between two to four hours then spray the top. (See Fig. 17 on the next page.)

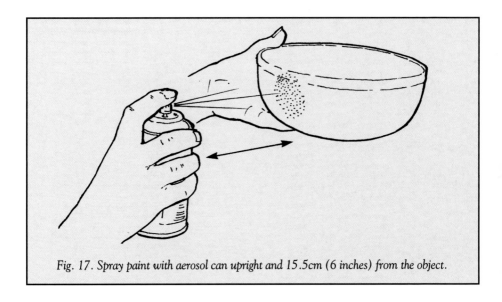

Fig. 17. Spray paint with aerosol can upright and 15.5cm (6 inches) from the object.

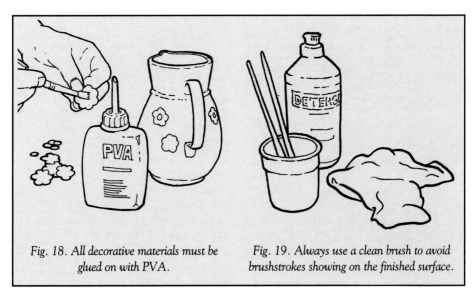

Fig. 18. All decorative materials must be glued on with PVA.

Fig. 19. Always use a clean brush to avoid brushstrokes showing on the finished surface.

STEP SEVEN
All items

After the decoration has been completed, varnishing will be the final process. Spirit-based polyurethane varnish is advizable for these particular objects. Once again, thoroughly check the handles, feet, surfaces and paint coverage to be absolutely sure you are ready for the varnish. Depending on the object, the inside may not need to be varnished. The jug, for example, will only need to be painted inside but the inside of the bowl will require a good coverage of varnish.

Paint the varnish in one direction, from top to bottom for instance, when applying the first coat, then from side to side with the next application. Insides and undersides should be the first surfaces to be covered and left to dry. Continue with the top sides and outsides for the next layer.

You will need between three to six coats of varnish, making sure you leave adequate drying periods in between, but it may take up to three months before your object is absolutely 'cured' after varnishing so be very careful with the completed work for this period of time. (Figs. 18 & 19.)

Congratulations, you have now created your own pieces of papier mâché. It is hoped that you will continue to enjoy this rewarding and absorbing hobby, creating many more beautiful and original objects with a little help from this book.

INDEX